BEYOND THE PAGES

CHALLENGING THE NOTION OF READING

ADHIRAJ NARANG

Made with ♥ on the Notion Press Platform
www.notionpress.com

To the past that shaped me, the present that nurtures me, and the future that awaits me.

Contents

Contents

Foreword

In a world where technology and digital media dominate our lives, the simple act of reading a book has taken on a whole new meaning. The traditional idea of flipping through pages and immersing oneself in a story seems to be fading away, replaced by quick snippets of information and instant gratification.

But amidst this changing landscape, there are those who dare to challenge the notion of reading. Adhiraj Narang's book, "Beyond The Pages," is a thought-provoking exploration of the power of literature and the transformative effect it can have on our lives.

In this captivating work, Adhiraj takes us on a journey beyond the surface-level experience of reading, delving into the depths of what it truly means to engage with a book. He challenges us to break free from the constraints of our fast-paced, technology-driven world and rediscover the joy of getting lost in the pages of a well-crafted story.

Through his personal anecdotes and insightful reflections, Adhiraj reminds us that reading is not merely a passive activity but an active process of self-discovery and growth. He explores how literature has the power to transport us to different worlds, expand our perspectives, and ignite our imagination.

But "Beyond The Pages" goes beyond just celebrating the joys of reading. Adhiraj also confronts the barriers that prevent us from fully embracing the literary world. He addresses the common excuses we make for not reading – lack of time, distractions, or simply not finding it enjoyable – and offers practical strategies to overcome these obstacles.

With his signature blend of warmth, humor, and wisdom, Adhiraj invites us to step out of our comfort zones and embark on a literary adventure. He encourages us to explore different genres, engage in meaningful discussions about books, and create spaces where reading is celebrated and cherished.

"Beyond The Pages" is not just a book; it is a call to action. It challenges us to reclaim our love for reading, to prioritize it amidst the chaos of our daily lives, and to recognize the profound impact it can have on our personal growth and understanding of the world.

So, dear reader, I invite you to join Adhiraj Narang on this transformative journey. Let us challenge the notion of reading and rediscover the magic that lies within the pages of a book. Together, let us embark on a quest to embrace literature, expand our horizons, and unlock the limitless possibilities that lie beyond the pages.

Preface

Writing "Beyond the Pages: Challenging the Notion of Reading has been a deeply personal and transformative journey for me. As I sat down to pen these words, I realized that I had been living my own life on the surface, never truly delving into the depths of my own story. It was time for a change.

This book is not just a collection of words on a page; it is a testament to the power of introspection and self-discovery. It is a reminder that we all have untold stories within us, waiting to be explored and embraced. It is my hope that by sharing my own experiences and insights, I can inspire others to embark on their own journeys of self-discovery.

Throughout the pages of this book, I invite you to join me as we navigate the intricacies of life and uncover the hidden narratives that shape our existence. Together, we will explore the uncharted territories of our hearts and minds, seeking a deeper connection with ourselves and the world around us.

I want to emphasize that this book is not a step-by-step guide to success or a one-size-fits-all solution to happiness. Rather, it is a gentle reminder to slow down, reflect, and embrace the beauty of life's unwritten stories. It is an invitation to live authentically, to savor every moment, and to find meaning in the seemingly mundane.

As you read these pages, I encourage you to engage with the practical exercises and reflect on your own experiences.

Allow yourself to question your assumptions, challenge your beliefs, and embrace the unknown with open arms. This journey is not always easy, but it is undoubtedly worth it.

I am immensely grateful for the opportunity to share my thoughts and insights with you through this book. I hope that it resonates with you on a deep level and encourages you to embark on your own journey of self-discovery.

Thank you for joining me on this extraordinary adventure. May "Beyond the Pages: Challenging the Notion of Reading" serve as a guiding light as you navigate the uncharted waters of your own existence. Together, let us embrace the untold stories that lie within us and live a life that goes beyond the pages.

About The Author

Adhiraj Narang, hailing from Punjab, is an author, actor, and philanthropist who has overcome personal challenges to create a meaningful and impactful life. During his school days, Adhiraj struggled with shyness, introversion, and low self-esteem. However, his life took a transformative turn when he shifted to Chandigarh and enrolled in Doon International School. This institution played a crucial role in nurturing his self-esteem and creativity, allowing him to blossom into the person he is today.

Motivated by his newfound confidence, Adhiraj delved into the world of theater, where he discovered a passion for acting. This newfound love for the stage inspired him to write his first book, "An Introvert Actor," during the challenging times of the Covid-19 pandemic. Through this book, Adhiraj shares his personal journey of overcoming introversion and how acting played a pivotal role in his personal growth.

Currently working as a cabin attendant with an international airline, Adhiraj continues to pursue his passion for storytelling and connecting with people. Alongside his flying career, he actively runs an NGO called Seva Foundation with his family. Through this organization, Adhiraj and his family strive to provide educational opportunities to underprivileged children, helping them build a brighter future.

Adhiraj's active presence on Instagram showcases his multifaceted personality. He collaborates with various brands, sharing his experiences and insights from his flying career. Additionally, he uses this platform to raise awareness about social causes and share glimpses of his philanthropic work.

Adhiraj Narang's life journey is a testament to the power of personal transformation and the impact one can make by embracing their passions and overcoming challenges. Through his writing, acting, and philanthropy, Adhiraj inspires others to break free from their limitations, pursue their dreams, and make a positive difference in the world.

CHAPTER ONE

The Limits of Imagination

The first chapter delves into the idea that reading books, while fostering imagination, can also inadvertently limit it. By relying solely on someone else's words and descriptions, readers may inadvertently stifle their own creative faculties. This chapter explores alternative ways to nurture imagination, such as engaging in hands-on activities, pursuing new experiences, and allowing the mind to wander freely.

Imagination is a powerful tool that allows us to explore the realms of possibility and create new worlds within our minds. It is through imagination that we can envision a future different from our present reality, dream up fantastical scenarios, and delve into the depths of our creativity. However, even with its boundless potential, there are limits to what our imagination can truly achieve.

One of the limits of imagination lies in its connection to our own experiences and knowledge. Our imagination is often shaped by what we have seen, heard, or read about in the world around us. While we can combine elements in new and unique ways, our imagination is ultimately limited by the boundaries of our own understanding. We can imagine creatures with wings, but they are still grounded in the concept of animals we have seen or heard of before. Our imagination is constrained by the familiar, making it difficult to truly conceive of something entirely outside of our realm of knowledge.

Another limit of imagination is its vulnerability to biases and preconceived notions. Our imagination is influenced by our beliefs, cultural background, and personal experiences. These biases can limit our ability to imagine beyond what we already know or believe to be true. We may struggle to imagine a world without poverty if we have never experienced it ourselves, or envision a society without discrimination if we have always lived within its confines. Our imagination is shaped by our own perspectives, making it challenging to transcend those limitations and truly imagine a different reality.

Furthermore, the limits of imagination are also evident in the practical constraints of the physical world. While we can imagine flying without wings or teleporting to distant lands, the laws of physics and the limitations of our human bodies prevent these imaginings from becoming a reality. We are bound by the constraints of time, space, and the natural laws that govern our existence. No matter how vividly we imagine something, there are certain limits to what can be achieved in the physical realm.

However, despite these limits, imagination remains a vital and transformative force in our lives. It allows us to dream, to envision a better future, and to push the boundaries of what is possible. While our imagination may be limited by our experiences, biases, and the constraints of reality, it still has the power to inspire, to innovate, and to spark change.

In conclusion, while there are limits to what our imagination can achieve, it is essential to recognize and embrace its potential. Our imagination may be shaped by our experiences and biases, and it may be constrained by the physical limitations of the world, but it still holds the power to ignite our creativity and push the boundaries of what we believe is possible. By acknowledging the limits of imagination, we can strive to expand our horizons, challenge our assumptions, and continue to explore the uncharted territories of our minds.

CHAPTER TWO

Breaking Free from Echo Chambers

Books often shape our perspectives, but they can also create echo chambers that limit our exposure to diverse ideas. This chapter discusses how reading books within our comfort zones can reinforce existing beliefs and prevent us from broadening our horizons. It encourages readers to seek out alternative sources of information, engage in dialogue with people from different backgrounds, and explore other mediums of knowledge dissemination.

In today's interconnected world, where information is readily available at our fingertips, it has become increasingly challenging to escape the clutches of echo chambers. Echo chambers refer to the phenomenon where individuals are surrounded by like-minded people and exposed only to information that reaffirms their existing beliefs and biases. This isolation from diverse perspectives can lead to a distorted understanding of reality, hinder critical thinking, and foster polarization within societies. To combat this issue, it is crucial for individuals to actively seek out diverse viewpoints, engage in open-minded discussions, and develop media literacy skills. In this essay, we will explore the detrimental effects of echo chambers, analyze the reasons behind their formation, and discuss strategies to break free from them.

The Detrimental Effects of Echo Chambers:

1. Polarization: Echo chambers contribute to the polarization of society by reinforcing existing beliefs and creating an "us versus them" mentality. When individuals are only exposed to opinions that align with their own, they become less willing to consider alternative perspectives. This lack of empathy and understanding can lead to increased hostility and division within communities.

2. Confirmation Bias: Echo chambers reinforce confirmation bias, which is the tendency to search for, interpret, and favor information that confirms preexisting beliefs. When people are surrounded by like-minded individuals who share similar views, they are more likely to dismiss or ignore contradictory evidence. This confirmation bias can hinder critical thinking and prevent individuals from making informed decisions.

3. Groupthink: Echo chambers can foster groupthink, a phenomenon where individuals conform to the opinions and decisions of the group without critically evaluating them. When people are constantly exposed to a narrow range of ideas, they may feel pressured to conform to the dominant narrative within their echo chamber. This conformity can stifle creativity, discourage dissenting opinions, and limit intellectual growth.

Reasons Behind the Formation of Echo Chambers:

1. Selective Exposure: Selective exposure is the tendency to seek out information that aligns with one's existing beliefs while avoiding contradictory viewpoints. In the age of personalized algorithms and social media, individuals are presented with content that caters to their preferences, further reinforcing their existing beliefs. This selective exposure creates a filter bubble, where individuals are shielded from diverse perspectives and alternative viewpoints.

2. Cognitive Dissonance: Cognitive dissonance is the discomfort experienced when confronted with conflicting ideas or information. To alleviate this discomfort, individuals may actively seek out information that supports their existing beliefs and avoid contradictory viewpoints. This cognitive dissonance avoidance can lead to the formation of echo chambers as people surround themselves with like-minded individuals who reaffirm their beliefs.

3. Social Identity: Humans have an innate desire to belong and be accepted by their social groups. Echo chambers provide a sense of belonging and validation, as individuals connect with like-minded people who share similar values and beliefs. This social identity reinforcement can create a strong emotional attachment to the echo chamber, making it difficult for individuals to break free from its grasp.

Strategies to Break Free from Echo Chambers:

1. Seek Diverse Perspectives: Actively seek out diverse perspectives by reading books, articles, and opinion pieces from various sources. Engage with individuals who hold different viewpoints in respectful and open-minded

discussions. By exposing ourselves to a range of opinions, we can broaden our understanding of complex issues and challenge our own biases.

2. Develop Media Literacy Skills: Enhance media literacy skills to critically evaluate the information we consume. Verify the credibility of sources,03:02

fact-check claims, and be aware of potential biases in the media we consume. By becoming informed consumers of information, we can avoid falling into echo chambers driven by misinformation and propaganda.

3. Encourage Civil Discourse: Foster an environment that encourages civil discourse and respectful dialogue. Engage in conversations with individuals who hold different opinions, focusing on understanding their perspectives rather than trying to change their minds. By promoting empathy and active listening, we can bridge divides and find common ground.

4. Embrace Cognitive Dissonance: Embrace cognitive dissonance as an opportunity for growth and learning. Instead of avoiding contradictory viewpoints, confront them head-on and critically evaluate the evidence. This willingness to challenge our own beliefs and engage with diverse perspectives can lead to personal growth and a more nuanced understanding of complex issues.

5. Divcrsify Social Networks: Actively diversify our social networks by seeking out individuals with different backgrounds, experiences, and opinions. Engage in activities or join communities that expose us to a diverse range of people. By expanding our social circles, we can

break out of our echo chambers and gain new insights into the world around us.

Conclusion:

Breaking free from echo chambers is essential for fostering a more inclusive, empathetic, and informed society. The detrimental effects of echo chambers, such as polarization, confirmation bias, and groupthink, highlight the urgency of addressing this issue. By actively seeking diverse perspectives, developing media literacy skills, encouraging civil discourse, embracing cognitive dissonance, and diversifying our social networks, we can break free from the confines of echo chambers. It is through these collective efforts that we can create a society that values critical thinking, empathy, and open-mindedness, ultimately leading to a more harmonious and well-informed world.03:02

CHAPTER THREE

The Art of Living

Life itself is a remarkable teacher, and this chapter highlights the importance of embracing real-world experiences over the solitary act of reading. It delves into the concept that true wisdom comes not from books alone but from actively engaging with the world around us. It explores the value of travel, human connections, and personal growth as essential components of a well-rounded life.

The Art of Living is a vast and intricate concept that encompasses various aspects of human existence. It is a philosophy, a way of life, and an ongoing journey towards self-discovery, personal growth, and fulfillment. The essence of this art lies in understanding and embracing the beauty, meaning, and purpose of life, as well as in cultivating wisdom, compassion, and gratitude.

At its core, the Art of Living revolves around the fundamental question of how to live a meaningful and fulfilling life. It recognizes that life is a precious gift, and every moment offers an opportunity for growth, learning, and transformation. It emphasizes the importance of living consciously, with awareness and intention, rather than merely existing on autopilot.

One of the key principles of the Art of Living is mindfulness. Mindfulness involves being fully present in the here and now, paying attention to our thoughts, feelings, and sensations without judgment. By cultivating mindfulness, we can develop a deep sense of self-awareness and gain insight into our own patterns of thinking, behaving, and relating to others.

Another essential aspect of the Art of Living is self-reflection. Taking time to reflect on our experiences, values, and beliefs allows us to gain clarity about who we are and what truly matters to us. Through self-reflection, we can uncover our passions, strengths, and purpose in life. It also enables us to recognize areas where we may need to grow or make changes in order to live more authentically and in alignment with our values.

The Art of Living also emphasizes the cultivation of virtues such as compassion, kindness, and gratitude. These virtues are considered essential for fostering healthy relationships, both with ourselves and with others. Compassion allows us to empathize with others' suffering and respond with kindness and understanding. Kindness enables us to extend goodwill and support to those around us. Gratitude helps us appreciate the blessings and opportunities that life presents us with.

In addition to these internal practices, the Art of Living also encompasses our interactions with the external world. It encourages us to live in harmony with nature and to be mindful of our impact on the environment. It emphasizes the importance of ethical behavior, integrity, and social responsibility. It calls us to cultivate empathy and to contribute positively to the well-being of our communities and the world at large.

The Art of Living recognizes that life is not without its challenges and hardships. It acknowledges that suffering is an inherent part of the human experience. However, it teaches us how to navigate through these difficulties with resilience, grace, and wisdom. It encourages us to embrace change, to let go of attachments and expectations, and to find meaning even in the midst of adversity.

Ultimately, the Art of Living is a lifelong journey of self-discovery, growth, and transformation. It is not a destination but rather a way of being in the world. It invites us to cultivate a deep sense of self-awareness, to live with intention and purpose, and to embrace the full spectrum of human experience. It reminds us that life is a precious gift, and that by fully engaging with it, we can create a life that is rich, meaningful, and fulfilling.

In conclusion, the Art of Living is a multifaceted concept that encompasses various principles, practices, and values aimed at living a meaningful and fulfilling life. It involves cultivating mindfulness, self-reflection, compassion, kindness, and gratitude. It emphasizes living in harmony with nature, ethical behavior, and social responsibility. It teaches us how to navigate through challenges with resilience and wisdom. Ultimately, it is a lifelong journey of self-discovery and personal growth. By embracing the Art of Living, we can create lives that are deeply fulfilling, purposeful, and aligned with our true selves.

CHAPTER FOUR

The Power of Conversation

Books are often solitary companions, but they lack the dynamic exchange of ideas that comes from engaging in conversations with others. This chapter explores the transformative power of dialogue, encouraging readers to seek out meaningful interactions, engage in debates, and challenge their own beliefs. It emphasizes the importance of active listening, empathy, and the ability to evolve through shared experiences.

The power of conversation is a profound and transformative force that shapes our relationships, influences our perspectives, and connects us to the world around us. Conversation is not simply the exchange of words; it is a dynamic and interactive process through which we share ideas, thoughts, emotions, and experiences. It is a fundamental aspect of human communication that has the ability to create understanding, build connections, and foster growth.

At its core, conversation is a means of connection. It is through conversation that we form relationships, establish bonds, and deepen our understanding of others.

Conversations allow us to share our thoughts, feelings, and experiences with one another, creating a sense of intimacy and connection. They provide a space for us to be seen, heard, and validated, fostering a sense of belonging and acceptance.

Conversation also plays a crucial role in shaping our perspectives and expanding our horizons. Through dialogue and discussion, we are exposed to new ideas, different viewpoints, and diverse experiences. Conversations challenge our assumptions, broaden our understanding, and encourage critical thinking. They enable us to question our own beliefs, consider alternative perspectives, and develop a more nuanced understanding of the world.

Furthermore, conversation is a powerful tool for personal growth and self-reflection. Engaging in meaningful conversations allows us to gain insights into ourselves, our values, and our aspirations. It provides an opportunity for self-expression and self-discovery, enabling us to explore our own thoughts and emotions more deeply. Through conversation, we can gain clarity about our own beliefs, values, and goals, helping us to live more authentically and in alignment with our true selves.

The power of conversation extends beyond the individual level; it has the potential to create positive change on a larger scale. Conversations can be catalysts for social change, fostering empathy, understanding, and collaboration. They have the ability to bridge divides, challenge prejudices, and promote inclusivity. Conversations can spark movements, inspire collective action, and drive social progress. They enable us to come together, share our stories, and work towards a more just and equitable society.

In addition to its interpersonal and societal impact, conversation also has profound effects on our mental and emotional well-being. Engaging in meaningful conversations can provide a sense of catharsis, allowing us to express our thoughts, emotions, and concerns. It can offer comfort, support, and validation, helping us to navigate through difficult times. Conversations can also be a source of inspiration, motivation, and encouragement, empowering us to overcome challenges and pursue our dreams.

The power of conversation lies not only in what is said, but also in how it is said. The tone, body language, and non-verbal cues all contribute to the impact of a conversation. Active listening, empathy, and respect are essential elements for effective communication. When we approach conversations with an open mind and a willingness to truly listen and understand, we create an environment that fosters trust, deepens connections, and encourages authentic dialogue.

Technology has revolutionized the way we communicate, providing us with new platforms and mediums for conversation. Social media, messaging apps, and video calls have made it easier than ever to connect with others across distances and time zones. However, it is important to recognize that these digital forms of communication have their limitations. While they offer convenience and accessibility, they often lack the depth, nuance, and intimacy of face-to-face conversations. In order to fully harness the power of conversation, it is important to prioritize in-person interactions and cultivate meaningful connections in our daily lives.

In conclusion, the power of conversation is a transformative force that shapes our relationships, influences our perspectives, and connects us to the world around us. It enables us to form connections, deepen understanding, and foster personal growth. Conversation has the potential to create positive change on both an individual and societal level. It plays a crucial role in shaping our perspectives, expanding our horizons, and promoting empathy and understanding. By embracing the power of conversation, we can cultivate meaningful connections, foster personal growth, and contribute to a more compassionate and inclusive world.

CHAPTER FIVE

The Unwritten Stories

The concept of unwritten stories refers to the untapped potential and possibilities that exist within each individual. It suggests that life is not predetermined or fixed, but rather a blank canvas waiting to be filled with unique experiences, accomplishments, and moments of joy. These unwritten stories represent the endless opportunities for growth, self-expression, and personal transformation that are available to everyone.

In a world that often emphasizes conformity and adhering to societal norms, embracing the beauty of unwritten stories is a radical act of self-empowerment and liberation. It challenges the notion that our lives are predetermined or limited by external circumstances, and instead encourages us to take control of our own narratives. By recognizing that we have the power to shape our own destinies, we can break free from the constraints of societal expectations and pursue a life that is true to our authentic selves.

Embracing the beauty of unwritten stories requires a willingness to step outside of our comfort zones and embrace uncertainty. It means taking risks, facing fears, and embracing the unknown. It requires us to let go of preconceived notions about what our lives should look like and instead embrace the possibilities that lie ahead. This can be both exhilarating and terrifying, as it requires us to confront our own limitations and push beyond them.

However, by embracing the beauty of unwritten stories, we open ourselves up to a world of endless possibilities. We become authors of our own lives, actively shaping our destinies and creating experiences that are meaningful and fulfilling. We no longer passively observe life from the sidelines, but rather actively participate in its creation.

Embracing the beauty of unwritten stories also requires a deep sense of self-awareness and introspection. It requires us to reflect on our values, passions, and aspirations, and align our actions with them. It means listening to our intuition and following our hearts, even when it may go against societal expectations or norms. It requires us to be true to ourselves, even in the face of adversity or criticism.

Furthermore, embracing the beauty of unwritten stories invites us to embrace imperfection and embrace failure as opportunities for growth and learning. It recognizes that setbacks and challenges are an inherent part of life's journey, and that they can ultimately lead to greater resilience and wisdom. By embracing failure as a stepping stone towards success, we can overcome obstacles and continue to write our own stories with courage and determination.

The beauty of unwritten stories lies not only in the individual, but also in the collective. Each person's unwritten story is interconnected with the stories of others, creating a tapestry of shared experiences and collective growth. By embracing the beauty of unwritten stories, we can foster connections and build communities that support and uplift one another. We can celebrate each other's successes, offer guidance in times of need, and create a more compassionate and inclusive world.

In conclusion, the beauty of unwritten stories lies in the limitless potential and possibilities that exist within each individual. By embracing the power to shape our own destinies, we can break free from societal constraints and pursue lives that are true to our authentic selves. Embracing the beauty of unwritten stories requires courage, self-awareness, and a willingness to embrace uncertainty. It invites us to step outside of our comfort zones, take risks, and actively participate in the creation of our own narratives. By embracing the beauty of unwritten stories, we can foster personal growth, create meaningful connections, and contribute to a more compassionate and inclusive world.

CHAPTER SIX

The Importance of Stepping Out in the Real World: Beyond Books

In today's digital age, where information is readily accessible at our fingertips, it is easy to get lost in the world of books and forget the importance of stepping out into the real world. While books offer a wealth of knowledge and insights, they can only provide a limited perspective and understanding of the world around us. Therefore, it is crucial to not just read books but also actively engage with the real world for a holistic and enriching experience.

Stepping out in the real world allows us to apply the knowledge we gain from books and put it into practice. It offers us the opportunity to test our theories, challenge our assumptions, and gain firsthand experiences that cannot be replicated through reading alone. By immersing ourselves in real-life situations, we can develop critical thinking skills, problem-solving abilities, and a deeper understanding of human nature.

Moreover, stepping out in the real world exposes us to diverse perspectives and cultures that we may not encounter within the pages of a book. It broadens our horizons, fosters empathy, and promotes tolerance and inclusivity. Interacting with people from different backgrounds and engaging in meaningful conversations allows us to break down stereotypes, challenge biases, and develop a more nuanced understanding of the world.

Additionally, the real world offers us the chance to develop essential life skills that cannot be learned solely through reading. Skills such as effective communication, adaptability, resilience, and teamwork are best honed through practical experiences and interactions with others. By actively engaging with the real world, we can cultivate these skills, which are invaluable in personal and professional settings.

Lastly, stepping out in the real world allows us to create lasting memories, forge meaningful connections, and find our own unique path in life. It offers us opportunities for personal growth, self-discovery, and the chance to pursue our passions and dreams. While books can inspire and provide guidance, it is through real-world experiences that we truly find ourselves and create a life that is authentic and fulfilling.

In conclusion, while books are valuable sources of knowledge and inspiration, they should not be the sole focus of our lives. Stepping out in the real world is essential for personal growth, gaining diverse perspectives, developing essential life skills, and creating meaningful connections. By striking a balance between reading and actively engaging with the world around us, we can lead a more enriching, fulfilling, and purposeful life.

CHAPTER SEVEN

But What If Books Did Not Exist?

If books were not there, the world would be a vastly different place. Books have been an essential part of human civilization for centuries, serving as a repository of knowledge, a source of inspiration, and a means of communication. They have shaped our understanding of the world, fueled our imagination, and facilitated the sharing of ideas across time and space. Without books, we would lose a fundamental tool for learning, growth, and cultural development.

Firstly, the absence of books would have a profound impact on education. Books are the primary medium through which knowledge is transmitted in schools and universities. They provide students with access to a wide range of subjects, from history and science to literature and philosophy. Without books, the educational system would need to rely solely on oral instruction or digital resources, which can be limited in terms of depth and accessibility. The absence of physical books would also mean the loss of libraries, which serve as vital community centers for learning and intellectual exploration.

Furthermore, books play a crucial role in preserving and disseminating cultural heritage. They capture the collective wisdom and experiences of past generations, allowing us to learn from their triumphs and failures. Through books, we can explore different cultures, traditions, and perspectives, fostering cross-cultural understanding and empathy. Without books, this rich tapestry of human knowledge and diversity would be lost or severely diminished. Oral traditions alone would struggle to preserve the vast array of stories, histories, and ideas that books offer.

In addition to their educational and cultural significance, books serve as a source of inspiration and escape. They transport us to different worlds, introduce us to fascinating characters, and ignite our imagination. Books provide solace during difficult times, offering comfort, guidance, and companionship. They allow us to explore our own emotions and experiences through the lens of others. Without books, we would lose a powerful medium for self-reflection, personal growth, and emotional connection.

Moreover, books have played a pivotal role in driving social change and promoting justice. Throughout history, books have been instrumental in challenging oppressive systems, advocating for human rights, and sparking revolutions. They have exposed injustices, inspired activism, and empowered marginalized communities. Without books, the voices of the oppressed and marginalized would be silenced, and the fight for equality and justice would be significantly hindered.

Furthermore, books provide a platform for intellectual

discourse and the exchange of ideas. They enable us to engage with different perspectives, challenge our own beliefs, and foster critical thinking. Books serve as a catalyst for innovation, sparking new ideas and discoveries. Without books, the intellectual development of society would be stifled, as the free flow of ideas would be severely restricted.

Additionally, books have economic value and contribute to the publishing industry. The absence of books would result in the loss of countless jobs in publishing, printing, distribution, and related fields. The book industry also supports independent bookstores, which are essential cultural hubs within communities. The disappearance of books would have far-reaching economic consequences.

Lastly, books hold sentimental value and serve as cherished heirlooms. They are often passed down through generations, carrying with them the memories, stories, and experiences of our ancestors. Books can evoke nostalgia, reminding us of significant moments in our lives or transporting us back to a specific time and place. Without books, we would lose a tangible connection to our past and the ability to pass on our own stories and knowledge to future generations.

In conclusion, the absence of books would have profound implications for education, culture, inspiration, social change, intellectual discourse, economy, and personal connections. Books are not just objects ade of paper and ink; they are vessels of knowledge, imagination, and human experience. They shape our understanding of the world, inspire us to dream and create, and connect us with others across time and space. Without books, our collective wisdom, cultural heritage, and intellectual development would be severely diminished. Therefore, we must cherish and celebrate the importance of books in our lives and ensure their continued presence in our ever-changing world.

CHAPTER EIGHT

The Power of Self-Reflection: Unlocking Your Full Potential through Self-Awareness

Unlocking our full potential is a lifelong journey of self-discovery, growth, and transformation. It requires a deep understanding of ourselves, our strengths, weaknesses, and aspirations. It demands commitment, perseverance, and a willingness to step outside our comfort zones. By embracing certain principles and practices, we can embark on this transformative path and unleash the boundless possibilities within us.

First and foremost, unlocking our full potential begins with self-awareness. We must take the time to explore our inner landscape, to understand our values, passions, and purpose. Self-reflection allows us to identify our unique talents and strengths, as well as areas for improvement. Through introspection, we gain clarity about who we are and what we want to achieve.

To unlock our full potential, we must set clear goals and create a roadmap for success. Goals provide direction and focus, allowing us to channel our energy towards meaningful endeavors. They should be specific, measurable, achievable, relevant, and time-bound (SMART). By breaking down our larger goals into smaller, manageable steps, we can make progress and stay motivated.

However, merely setting goals is not enough; we must also cultivate discipline and consistency. Consistent effort and commitment are essential in realizing our potential. It requires developing healthy habits and routines that align with our objectives. Whether it's dedicating regular time for learning, practicing a skill, or pursuing personal growth, consistency builds momentum and propels us forward.

Moreover, unlocking our full potential necessitates embracing a growth mindset. A growth mindset is the belief that our abilities and intelligence can be developed through dedication and hard work. It encourages us to view challenges as opportunities for growth rather than setbacks. With a growth mindset, we approach obstacles with resilience and perseverance, recognizing that failures are stepping stones towards success.

To unlock our full potential, we must also cultivate a positive mindset. Our thoughts and beliefs shape our reality and influence our actions. By adopting a positive outlook, we can overcome self-doubt, fear, and limiting beliefs that hold us back. Positive affirmations, visualization, and gratitude practices can help reframe our thinking and foster a mindset of abundance and possibility.

Furthermore, unlocking our full potential requires continuous learning and personal development. We must be open to acquiring new knowledge, skills, and perspectives. Reading books, attending workshops, seeking mentors, and engaging in lifelong learning enable us to expand our horizons and stay adaptable in an ever-changing world. Embracing a growth mindset also encourages us to view feedback as an opportunity for improvement and to seek constructive criticism.

In addition to personal development, unlocking our full potential necessitates building a strong support network. Surrounding ourselves with positive, like-minded individuals who believe in our potential can provide encouragement, accountability, and inspiration. Collaborating with others allows us to leverage collective wisdom and resources, fostering innovation and growth. Seeking out mentors and role models who have achieved what we aspire to can provide valuable guidance and insights.

To unlock our full potential, it is crucial to cultivate resilience and embrace failure as a stepping stone to success. Failure is an inevitable part of any journey towards growth and achievement. It teaches us valuable lessons, builds character, and strengthens our resolve. By reframing failure as an opportunity for learning and growth, we can bounce back stronger and more determined than before.

Moreover, unlocking our full potential requires embracing discomfort and stepping outside our comfort zones. Growth occurs when we challenge ourselves and take calculated risks. By embracing new experiences, confronting our fears, and pushing past our perceived limits, we expand our capabilities and discover hidden talents. Stepping outside our comfort zones fosters personal growth, resilience, and adaptability.

To unlock our full potential, it is essential to prioritize self-care and well-being. Taking care of our physical, mental, and emotional health is crucial for sustained growth and optimal performance. Engaging in regular exercise, maintaining a balanced diet, practicing mindfulness, and nurturing meaningful relationships contribute to our overall well-being. When we prioritize self-care, we have the energy, focus, and resilience needed to unlock our full potential.

Furthermore, unlocking our full potential requires perseverance and a willingness to embrace setbacks as opportunities for growth. It is important to remain patient and persistent, understanding that progress may not always be linear. The path to realizing our potential may be filled with challenges, detours, and moments of self-doubt. However, by staying committed to our goals and maintaining a positive mindset, we can overcome obstacles and continue moving forward.

In conclusion, unlocking our full potential is a lifelong journey that requires self-awareness, goal setting, discipline, a growth mindset, continuous learning, building a support network, embracing failure and discomfort, prioritizing self-care, and perseverance. By embracing these principles and practices, we can tap into our limitless potential and lead a fulfilling and purposeful life. It is through unlocking our full potential that we contribute to the betterment of ourselves, our communities, and the world at large.

self-reflection

Self-reflection is the process of examining one's thoughts, emotions, and actions in order to gain a deeper understanding of oneself. It involves introspection, self-analysis, and self-examination. Self-reflection is significant because it allows individuals to become more self-aware and make conscious choices about their behaviors and decisions.

Through self-reflection, individuals can gain insights into their values, beliefs, and motivations. It helps them understand why they think, feel, and act the way they do. Self-reflection also enables individuals to identify their strengths and weaknesses, allowing them to capitalize on their strengths and work on areas for improvement.

Additionally, self-reflection plays a crucial role in personal growth and development. It allows individuals to learn from their past experiences and mistakes, leading to increased resilience and adaptability. By reflecting on their actions and decisions, individuals can make adjustments and develop new strategies for success.

Self-reflection is not only beneficial on an individual level but also has broader implications. When individuals are self-aware and understand themselves better, they can build stronger relationships, communicate more effectively, and contribute positively to their communities. Self-reflection also promotes empathy and understanding towards others, fostering a more compassionate and inclusive society. Overall, self-reflection is a powerful tool for unlocking one's full potential and living a purposeful and fulfilling life.

How self-reflection enhances self-awareness

Self-reflection enhances self-awareness by providing individuals with the opportunity to examine their thoughts, emotions, and actions objectively. It allows them to step back and observe themselves from a more detached perspective. Through self-reflection, individuals can gain a deeper understanding of their values, beliefs, and motivations, which ultimately contributes to a greater sense of self-awareness.

Self-reflection helps individuals become aware of their patterns of thinking and behavior. It allows them to identify recurring thoughts, emotions, and actions that may be hindering their personal growth or causing negative outcomes. By recognizing these patterns, individuals can take steps to change them and make more conscious choices.

Self-reflection also helps individuals become aware of their strengths and weaknesses. By reflecting on their actions and experiences, individuals can identify areas where they excel and areas where they may need improvement. This awareness allows individuals to capitalize on their strengths and work on developing skills in areas that require growth.

Furthermore, self-reflection promotes a deeper

understanding of one's emotions. It allows individuals to explore the underlying reasons behind their feelings and reactions. By examining their emotions, individuals can gain insight into their triggers and develop strategies for managing them more effectively.

Overall, self-reflection enhances self-awareness by providing individuals with the opportunity to observe themselves objectively, recognize patterns of thinking and behavior, identify strengths and weaknesses, and gain a deeper understanding of their emotions. This increased self-awareness enables individuals to make more informed choices and live a more authentic and fulfilling life.

The role of self-reflection in identifying strengths, weaknesses, and aspirations

Self-reflection plays a crucial role in identifying strengths, weaknesses, and aspirations. When individuals engage in self-reflection, they have the opportunity to assess their abilities and areas for improvement objectively.

By reflecting on their actions and experiences, individuals can identify their strengths. They can recognize the skills and qualities that they excel in and leverage them to achieve their goals. This awareness of strengths allows individuals to capitalize on their abilities and pursue opportunities that align with their talents.

On the other hand, self-reflection also helps individuals identify their weaknesses. By examining their thoughts, emotions, and actions, individuals can become aware of areas where they may need improvement. This self-awareness allows them to take steps to develop these areas and work towards personal growth.

Self-reflection also aids in identifying aspirations. By reflecting on their values, beliefs, and motivations, individuals can gain clarity on what they truly desire in life. They can identify their long-term goals and aspirations, whether it be in their career, relationships, or personal development. This awareness of aspirations provides individuals with a sense of direction and purpose, guiding their decisions and actions towards achieving their desired outcomes.

In summary, self-reflection plays a vital role in identifying strengths, weaknesses, and aspirations. It allows individuals to objectively assess their abilities, recognize areas for improvement, and gain clarity on their long-term goals. This self-awareness enables individuals to make informed choices and take steps towards personal growth and fulfillment.

CHAPTER NINE

Techniques for Effective Self-Reflection

1. Journaling: Write down your thoughts, feelings, and experiences regularly in a journal. This helps you gain clarity and insight into your actions and emotions.

2. Meditation: Set aside time for quiet reflection and mindfulness. Focus on your thoughts and emotions without judgment, allowing yourself to become more self-aware.

3. Seeking feedback: Ask for feedback from trusted friends, family members, or mentors. Their perspectives can provide valuable insights into your strengths and weaknesses.

4. Asking reflective questions: Challenge yourself with questions that prompt deeper thinking, such as "What did I learn from this experience?" or "What could I have done differently?"

5. Setting goals: Reflect on your aspirations and set specific, measurable goals to work towards. This helps you stay focused and motivated on your desired outcomes.

6. Self-assessment tools: Utilize self-assessment tools or personality tests to gain a better understanding of your strengths, weaknesses, and preferences.

7. Reflecting on past experiences: Look back on past successes and failures and analyze what contributed to each outcome. This helps you identify patterns and areas for improvement.

8. Seeking professional help: If needed, consider working with a therapist or coach who can provide guidance and support in your self-reflection journey.

Remember, self-reflection is an ongoing process that requires time and commitment. By regularly engaging in self-reflection techniques, you can continue to grow, develop, and achieve your goals.

Journaling

Journaling: Write down your thoughts, feelings, and experiences regularly in a journal. This helps you gain clarity and insight into your actions and emotions.

Meditation: Set aside time for quiet reflection and mindfulness. Focus on your thoughts and emotions without judgment, allowing yourself to become more self-aware.

Seeking feedback: Ask for feedback from trusted friends, family members, or mentors. Their perspectives can provide valuable insights into your strengths and weaknesses.

Asking reflective questions: Challenge yourself with questions that prompt deeper thinking, such as "What did I learn from this experience?" or "What could I have done differently?"

Setting goals: Reflect on your aspirations and set specific, measurable goals to work towards. This helps you stay focused and motivated on your desired outcomes.

Self-assessment tools: Utilize self-assessment tools or personality tests to gain a better understanding of your strengths, weaknesses, and preferences.

Reflecting on past experiences: Look back on past successes and failures and analyze what contributed to each outcome. This helps you identify patterns and areas for improvement.

Seeking professional help: If needed, consider working with a therapist or coach who can provide guidance and support in your self-reflection journey.

Remember, self-reflection is an ongoing process that requires time and commitment. By regularly engaging in self-reflection techniques, you can continue to grow, develop, and achieve your goals.

Meditation

Set aside time for quiet reflection and mindfulness. Focus on your thoughts and emotions without judgment, allowing yourself to become more self-aware.

Meditation is a powerful tool for self-reflection and self-awareness. By setting aside dedicated time for quiet reflection and mindfulness, you can create a space to observe your thoughts and emotions without judgment.

During meditation, you can focus on your breath or a specific mantra to help anchor your attention. As thoughts or emotions arise, simply notice them without getting caught up in them or judging them as good or bad. This practice allows you to develop a greater sense of self-awareness and understanding.

Through regular meditation, you can cultivate a deeper connection with yourself, gain clarity on your values and priorities, and develop a greater sense of inner peace and calm. It can also help you become more present in your daily life and improve your ability to respond to challenges with mindfulness and intention.

Remember that meditation is a skill that takes time and practice to develop. Start with just a few minutes each day and gradually increase the duration as you become more comfortable. Experiment with different techniques and find what works best for you.

Overall, meditation is a valuable tool for self-reflection and personal growth. By incorporating it into your routine, you can enhance your self-awareness and create a foundation for continued self-improvement.

Seeking feedback

Ask for feedback from trusted friends, family members, or mentors. Their perspectives can provide valuable insights into your strengths and weaknesses.

Additionally, consider seeking feedback from meditation instructors or experienced practitioners. They can offer guidance on your technique and provide suggestions for improvement.

When asking for feedback, be open and receptive to constructive criticism. Remember that the goal is to grow and develop, so any feedback should be seen as an opportunity for growth rather than a personal attack.

It can also be helpful to keep a journal or record of your meditation practice. This allows you to track your progress over time and reflect on any patterns or insights that arise during your sessions. By reviewing your journal entries, you may discover areas where you can further refine your practice.

Ultimately, the feedback you receive can help you deepen your self-reflection and enhance your meditation practice. Embrace the opportunity to learn and grow, and continue to explore different techniques and approaches to find what resonates with you personally.

Conclusion:

By embracing the power of self-reflection, we can embark on a transformative journey towards unlocking our full potential. It is through self-awareness and deep introspection that we gain clarity, identify our strengths and weaknesses, and set meaningful goals. Self-reflection allows us to grow, adapt, and become the best versions of ourselves. Ultimately, unlocking our full potential through self-reflection not only benefits us but also contributes to the betterment of our communities and the world as a whole.

CHAPTER TEN

Successful Individuals But No Books

There have been successful individuals who have achieved great things without reading books extensively. While reading can provide valuable knowledge and insights, it is not the only path to success. Here are a few reasons why some successful people may not prioritize reading books:

1. Practical Experience: Some individuals learn best through hands-on experience and real-life situations. They may prefer to learn by doing rather than reading about it in a book.

2. Alternative Learning Methods: Successful people may have found alternative ways to acquire knowledge and skills, such as through mentorship, practical training, or experiential learning programs. They may prioritize these methods over reading books.

3. Focus on Action: Some individuals believe that taking action and implementing ideas is more important than consuming information from books. They may prefer to spend their time actively pursuing their goals rather than

reading about them.

4. Personal Preferences: Reading may simply not be a preferred method of learning for some successful individuals. They may find other mediums, such as podcasts, documentaries, or online courses, more engaging and effective for acquiring knowledge.

5. Time Constraints: Successful people often have demanding schedules and limited time for leisure activities like reading. They may prioritize other activities that they find more directly beneficial to their success.

It's important to note that while reading books may not be a priority for some successful individuals, they still value continuous learning and personal growth. They may seek knowledge and insights through different means, such as networking, attending conferences, or engaging in meaningful conversations with experts in their field.

Ultimately, the key to success lies in finding what works best for you as an individual. While reading books can be valuable, it is not the sole determinant of success. It's important to explore various learning methods and find the approach that resonates with your learning style and goals.

CHAPTER ELEVEN

Practical Experience

The debate between practical experience and reading books is a subjective one, as both have their own merits and can be valuable in different ways.

Practical experience allows individuals to gain firsthand knowledge and skills through direct involvement in real-life situations. It provides a deeper understanding of concepts and allows for the application of theoretical knowledge in a practical setting. Practical experience also helps individuals develop problem-solving skills, adaptability, and resilience, as they encounter challenges and learn how to overcome them.

On the other hand, reading books offers a wealth of information and insights from experts in various fields. Books provide a platform for learning from the experiences and wisdom of others, allowing individuals to gain knowledge without having to go through the same trials and errors themselves. Books also offer the opportunity to explore different perspectives, theories, and ideas that may not be readily available in one's immediate environment.

Ultimately, the value of practical experience versus reading books depends on the context and the individual's goals. In some fields, such as medicine or engineering, practical experience is crucial for developing technical skills and expertise. In other areas, such as philosophy or history, reading books can provide a solid foundation of knowledge and critical thinking skills.

Ideally, a combination of practical experience and reading books can be the most effective approach. Practical experience provides the opportunity for hands-on learning and skill development, while reading books enhances one's understanding, broadens perspectives, and allows for continuous learning and growth.

In Adhiraj Narang's case, his diverse background and experiences in theater, philanthropy, and writing likely combine both practical experience and reading books. His practical experience as a theater actor allowed him to develop his acting skills and understand the power of storytelling firsthand. However, his passion for continuous learning and exploration led him to write a book, where he shares inspiring anecdotes and insights to empower readers. This suggests that he recognizes the value of both practical experience and reading books in his personal growth and pursuit of making a positive impact on the world.

CHAPTER TWELVE

Alternative Learning Methods

Apart from reading books, there are several alternative learning methods that individuals can utilize to gain knowledge and skills:

1. Online courses: With the advancement of technology, online courses have become increasingly popular. Platforms like Coursera, Udemy, and Khan Academy offer a wide range of courses on various subjects, allowing individuals to learn at their own pace and from the comfort of their own homes.

2. Workshops and seminars: Attending workshops and seminars provides an opportunity to learn from experts in a specific field. These events often involve interactive sessions, discussions, and practical exercises that enhance learning and skill development.

3. Mentoring and apprenticeships: Finding a mentor or participating in an apprenticeship program allows individuals to learn directly from experienced professionals. Mentors can provide guidance, advice, and

real-world insights that may not be found in books.

4. Hands-on projects: Engaging in hands-on projects and practical applications of knowledge can be an effective way to learn. This could involve building something, conducting experiments, or solving real-life problems.

5. Experiential learning: Experiential learning involves learning through direct experience and reflection. This could include internships, volunteering, or participating in community service projects.

6. Podcasts and audiobooks: Listening to podcasts or audiobooks can be an alternative to reading books. These mediums provide access to expert interviews, discussions, and storytelling that can enhance learning and understanding.

7. Online forums and communities: Participating in online forums or joining communities related to a specific topic allows individuals to engage in discussions, ask questions, and learn from others who share similar interests.

8. Visual and multimedia resources: Utilizing visual and multimedia resources such as videos, documentaries, infographics, and interactive websites can provide a more engaging and dynamic learning experience.

It is important to note that different individuals may have different preferences and learning styles. Therefore, it is beneficial to explore and experiment with various alternative learning methods to find the ones that work best for individual needs and goals.

CHAPTER THIRTEEN

Focus on Action

These individuals may prioritize hands-on experiences, practical projects, and real-life applications of knowledge. They believe that true learning happens through action and that taking risks and making mistakes is an essential part of the learning process.

For these individuals, alternative learning methods such as workshops, apprenticeships, and experiential learning opportunities are highly valuable. They seek out opportunities to apply their knowledge in real-world settings, whether through internships, volunteering, or participating in community service projects.

Additionally, they may find podcasts and audiobooks useful as they can listen to expert interviews and discussions while engaging in other activities. This allows them to continue learning and gaining insights even while on the go or during tasks that do not require their full attention.

Online forums and communities also play a crucial role for these individuals as they provide a platform for sharing ideas, seeking advice, and learning from others who have similar interests or goals. Engaging in discussions and asking questions allows them to gain different perspectives and expand their understanding of a particular topic.

Visual and multimedia resources are also highly effective for these individuals as they provide a more dynamic and engaging learning experience. Videos, documentaries, infographics, and interactive websites can bring concepts to life and make them easier to understand and remember.

Ultimately, for individuals who prioritize action and implementation, alternative learning methods that involve active participation, practical application, and real-world experiences are key. They believe that true learning happens through doing rather than just consuming information, and they seek out opportunities to put their knowledge into practice.

CHAPTER FOURTEEN

Personal Preferences

These individuals may prefer to learn through listening rather than reading. They may find that podcasts and audiobooks allow them to absorb information while multitasking or engaging in other activities. They can listen to expert interviews, discussions, and educational content, gaining insights and expanding their knowledge even while on the go.

Documentaries and videos may also be highly effective for these individuals. They provide a visual and immersive learning experience, bringing concepts to life and making them easier to understand and remember. Visual learners may particularly benefit from these resources as they can see demonstrations, examples, and real-world applications of the knowledge they are acquiring.

Online courses and workshops may be preferred over traditional classroom settings for these individuals. They value hands-on experiences and practical projects, and alternative learning methods such as experiential learning opportunities or apprenticeships may be highly valuable to them. They seek out opportunities to apply their knowledge in real-world settings, whether through internships, volunteering, or participating in community service projects.

Engaging with online forums and communities is also important for these individuals. They value the opportunity to share ideas, seek advice, and learn from others who have similar interests or goals. Participating in discussions and asking questions allows them to gain different perspectives and expand their understanding of a particular topic.

In summary, individuals who prioritize action and implementation may find alternative learning methods such as podcasts, documentaries, online courses, and experiential learning opportunities more engaging and effective than traditional reading. They value hands-on experiences, practical projects, and real-life applications of knowledge, believing that true learning happens through action and taking risks.

CHAPTER FIFTEEN

Time Constraints

For these individuals, alternative learning methods such as podcasts and audiobooks can be a valuable tool. They can listen to these resources while commuting, exercising, or doing household chores, maximizing their time and allowing them to learn while on the go. This way, they can continue to expand their knowledge and stay up to date with industry trends without sacrificing their other commitments.

Documentaries and videos also cater to their time constraints as they provide a visual and immersive learning experience that can be consumed in shorter periods. Instead of dedicating hours to reading a book, they can watch a documentary or video that covers the same topic in a fraction of the time. This allows them to quickly grasp key concepts and gain valuable insights without spending excessive amounts of time.

Online courses and workshops are another effective option for individuals with time constraints. These learning platforms often offer flexible schedules and self-paced learning, allowing busy individuals to fit their education around their existing commitments. They can access course materials at their convenience and complete assignments or projects when it suits them best.

Engaging with online forums and communities also fits well into their time constraints. They can participate in discussions and seek advice whenever they have a spare moment, without needing to commit to specific meeting times or lengthy conversations. This way, they can still benefit from the knowledge and insights of others without having to dedicate large chunks of time.

In conclusion, alternative learning methods such as podcasts, documentaries, online courses, and online communities are ideal for individuals with time constraints. These methods allow them to make the most of their limited leisure time and continue their learning journey without sacrificing their other commitments.

CHAPTER SIXTEEN

Non-Fiction Books

Reading non-fiction books is important for several reasons:

1. Knowledge and Learning: Non-fiction books provide valuable information and knowledge on a wide range of topics. They cover subjects such as history, science, philosophy, self-improvement, and more. By reading non-fiction, you can expand your understanding of the world and gain insights into different subjects.

2. Personal Growth: Non-fiction books often offer practical advice, strategies, and insights that can help you grow personally and professionally. They can provide guidance on topics such as leadership, communication, time management, and goal-setting. Reading non-fiction books allows you to learn from the experiences and expertise of others.

3. Critical Thinking and Analysis: Non-fiction books challenge your thinking and encourage critical analysis. They present arguments, evidence, and different perspectives on various topics, which can help you develop your own critical thinking skills. Reading non-fiction helps you become a more informed and analytical thinker.

4. Empathy and Understanding: Non-fiction books often delve into the lives and experiences of real people. They can provide insights into different cultures, societies, and human experiences. By reading non-fiction, you can develop empathy and a better understanding of the world around you.

5. Stay Informed: Non-fiction books keep you up to date with current events, trends, and developments in different fields. They offer in-depth analysis and research on various topics, helping you stay informed and knowledgeable about the world.

6. Language and Vocabulary Development: Reading non-fiction books exposes you to a wide range of vocabulary and language usage. It helps improve your reading comprehension, language skills, and overall communication abilities.

Overall, reading non-fiction books is essential for personal growth, knowledge acquisition, critical thinking, empathy development, and staying informed. It allows you to explore new ideas, broaden your horizons, and continuously learn throughout your life.

CHAPTER SEVENTEEN

My Favourite Topic: Backbenchers

There is no definitive answer to why backbenchers and failure students sometimes become more successful in life than toppers. Success in life is influenced by various factors such as determination, resilience, creativity, adaptability, and networking skills. Here are a few possible reasons:

1. Different Perspectives: Backbenchers and failure students may have a different perspective on education and life. They may question traditional methods, think outside the box, and explore unconventional paths. This mindset can lead to innovative ideas and approaches that contribute to their success.

2. Resilience and Perseverance: Failure students often face setbacks and challenges throughout their academic journey. These experiences can build resilience and teach them how to overcome obstacles. This resilience can translate into their professional lives, allowing them to handle setbacks and failures with a positive attitude.

3. Outside-the-Box Thinking: Toppers often excel at

following rules and meeting expectations, while backbenchers may have a more rebellious nature. This can lead to creative thinking and problem-solving abilities that are valuable in many industries. Backbenchers may be more willing to take risks and try new approaches, leading to unique opportunities for success.

4. Networking and Social Skills: While academic success is important, success in life often requires strong networking and social skills. Backbenchers and failure students may have spent more time building relationships, connecting with people from diverse backgrounds, and developing interpersonal skills. These skills can be crucial for career advancement and opportunities.

5. Passion and Drive: Sometimes, failure students or backbenchers have a deep passion for a particular field or interest that drives them to succeed. Their passion can fuel their motivation and dedication to their chosen path, leading to greater success in the long run.

6. Entrepreneurial Spirit: Backbenchers may possess an entrepreneurial spirit and be more willing to take risks or start their own businesses. Entrepreneurship can provide higher earning potential if successful.

7. Industry Demand: Some industries may value practical experience or specific skill sets over academic achievements. Backbenchers may have gained relevant experience or specialized knowledge that is in high demand, leading to higher-paying job opportunities.

8. Negotiation Skills: Backbenchers may have developed strong negotiation skills through their experiences with setbacks and challenges. These skills can be beneficial when negotiating salaries or promotions, potentially

leading to higher earnings.

It's important to note that success is subjective and can be defined differently by individuals. The reasons mentioned above are general observations and may not apply to every situation. Ultimately, success in life depends on a combination of various factors, including personal circumstances, opportunities, and individual choices.

CHAPTER EIGHTEEN

Low self-esteem individuals

Low self-esteem individuals can still find success in life without reading books by focusing on other areas and strategies. Here are a few suggestions:

1. Identify Strengths: Everyone has unique strengths and talents. By identifying these strengths and focusing on developing them, individuals can excel in their chosen fields without relying solely on reading books.

2. Practical Experience: Gaining hands-on experience through internships, volunteering, or apprenticeships can provide valuable knowledge and skills that are applicable in real-life situations. This practical experience can be just as valuable, if not more, than theoretical knowledge gained from books.

3. Networking and Mentoring: Building a strong network of supportive individuals can provide guidance, advice, and opportunities for growth. Seeking out mentors who have achieved success in their respective fields can be particularly helpful in gaining insights and learning from

their experiences.

4. Continuous Learning: While reading books may not be the preferred method for some individuals, there are alternative ways to continue learning. This can include attending workshops, seminars, online courses, or participating in practical training programs that focus on hands-on learning.

5. Embrace Failure and Learn from Setbacks: Success often comes with its fair share of failures and setbacks. Low self-esteem individuals can find success by embracing these failures as learning opportunities, adapting their strategies, and persisting through challenges.

6. Set Goals and Take Action: Setting specific goals and taking consistent action towards achieving them is crucial for success. By breaking down larger goals into smaller, manageable steps, individuals can make progress and build confidence along the way.

It's important to remember that success is subjective and can be defined differently by each individual. While reading books can provide valuable knowledge and insights, it is not the only path to success. By focusing on personal strengths, practical experiences, networking, continuous learning, resilience, and goal-setting, individuals with low self-esteem can still find success in various aspects of life.

CHAPTER NINETEEN

A Short Story

Once upon a time, in a small town called Oakwood, there lived a young woman named Lily. Lily had always struggled with low self-esteem, often feeling inadequate compared to her peers who seemed to excel in various areas of life. She believed that her lack of interest in reading books was holding her back from achieving success.

One day, as Lily sat in the local park, feeling lost and discouraged, she noticed a group of children playing soccer. Intrigued by their enthusiasm and skill, she decided to join them. To her surprise, Lily discovered that she had a natural talent for the sport. She quickly became an integral part of the team, leading them to victory in several matches.

Through her involvement in soccer, Lily realized the importance of identifying her strengths. She embraced her athletic abilities and started focusing on developing them further. She attended training sessions, joined local leagues, and even began coaching younger children. Lily found immense joy and fulfillment in her newfound passion.

As she continued to immerse herself in the world of sports,

Lily also recognized the value of practical experience. She sought out internships with professional sports teams and volunteered at community events. This hands-on experience provided her with valuable knowledge and skills that were applicable in real-life situations.

However, Lily's journey towards success didn't stop there. She understood the importance of building a strong network and seeking guidance from mentors. Through her involvement in sports, she met coaches and athletes who became her mentors. They shared their experiences, provided advice, and opened doors to new opportunities. Lily realized that success was not just about individual achievements but also about the support and guidance of others.

Although reading books wasn't her preferred method of learning, Lily continued to pursue knowledge through alternative means. She attended workshops and seminars on sports psychology, nutrition, and leadership. She participated in practical training programs that allowed her to learn hands-on skills relevant to her field.

Along her path to success, Lily faced numerous setbacks and failures. However, she refused to let them define her. Instead, she embraced these challenges as learning opportunities. Each failure taught her valuable lessons, enabling her to adapt her strategies and persist through adversity.

With each small victory, Lily gained confidence and began setting specific goals for herself. She broke down her larger aspirations into smaller, manageable steps, taking consistent action towards achieving them. Whether it was improving her skills, mentoring others, or pursuing higher education in sports management, Lily remained focused and determined.

As the years went by, Lily's dedication and hard work paid off. She became a renowned sports coach, helping countless athletes reach their full potential. Her story inspired many individuals with low self-esteem, showing them that success could be achieved beyond the pages of a book.

Lily's journey taught her that success is subjective and can be defined differently by each individual. She realized that while reading books can provide valuable knowledge, it is not the sole path to success. By focusing on personal strengths, practical experiences, networking, continuous learning, resilience, and goal-setting, individuals with low self-esteem can still find success in various aspects of life.

And so, Lily's story became a testament to the fact that success is not limited to the pages of a book but can be found in the pursuit of one's passions and the belief in oneself.

Incorporating reading

Reading books as an adult has numerous benefits that can contribute to personal growth and success. Here are a few reasons why you should consider reading books:

1. Knowledge and Learning: Books are a treasure trove of knowledge, ideas, and information. They provide an opportunity to learn about new subjects, explore different perspectives, and expand your understanding of the world. Reading books allows you to gain insights and expertise in various areas, which can be valuable in both personal and professional contexts.

2. Cognitive Development: Reading stimulates the brain and improves cognitive functions such as memory, concentration, and critical thinking. It enhances vocabulary, language skills, and communication abilities. Regular reading can also improve analytical and problem-solving skills, helping you approach challenges more effectively.

3. Emotional Intelligence: Books often delve into complex human emotions and experiences, allowing readers to develop empathy and emotional intelligence. Through stories and characters, books provide insights into different cultures, perspectives, and life situations, fostering greater understanding and compassion.

4. Stress Reduction and Relaxation: Reading can be a great

way to unwind and relax after a long day. It helps reduce stress levels by diverting attention from daily worries and immersing you in a different world. Reading before bed can also promote better sleep and relaxation.

5. Improved Focus and Concentration: In today's digital age of constant distractions, reading books can help improve focus and concentration. Engaging with a book requires sustained attention, allowing you to develop the ability to concentrate for longer periods.

6. Personal Growth and Self-Reflection: Books often contain valuable insights and life lessons that can contribute to personal growth and self-reflection. They can inspire you to reflect on your own beliefs, values, and experiences, leading to self-discovery and personal development.

7. Enhanced Communication Skills: Reading books exposes you to different writing styles, vocabulary, and storytelling techniques. This exposure can enhance your own writing and communication skills, enabling you to express yourself more effectively in various contexts.

8. Mental Stimulation and Brain Health: Reading regularly has been linked to improved brain health and a reduced risk of cognitive decline. It keeps the brain active, engaged, and stimulated, promoting mental agility and overall well-being.

While Lily's story shows that success can be achieved

without a strong interest in reading books, it is important to recognize the unique benefits that reading can offer. Incorporating reading into your life can complement other pursuits and contribute to personal and professional growth.

CHAPTER TWENTY

Books In Future

While it is difficult to predict the future with certainty, it is highly likely that people will continue to read books in some form. Books have been a source of knowledge, entertainment, and inspiration for centuries, and they hold a unique place in our cultural heritage.

Although technology has introduced new ways to consume information and stories, such as e-books and audiobooks, the experience of reading a physical book still holds value for many people. The tactile sensation of turning pages, the smell of ink and paper, and the ability to disconnect from screens and distractions are all aspects that contribute to the enduring appeal of books.

Furthermore, books offer a depth and richness that can be challenging to replicate in other mediums. They allow readers to engage with ideas, characters, and narratives in a way that encourages imagination and critical thinking.

While the way we consume books may evolve in the future, it is likely that the act of reading itself will continue to be cherished by individuals seeking knowledge, entertainment, and personal growth.

what readers can potentially learn from books like "Beyond the Pages: Embracing Life's Unwritten Stories" by Adhiraj Narang.

1. Embracing uncertainty: The book may explore the idea of embracing the unknown and finding beauty in life's unpredictable moments. It could encourage readers to let go of rigid expectations and embrace the unexpected turns that life takes.

2. Self-discovery and personal growth: Books like this often delve into the journey of self-discovery and personal growth. They may offer insights and reflections on how to navigate through life's challenges, find one's purpose, and develop a deeper understanding of oneself.

3. Resilience and overcoming obstacles: The book might share stories or anecdotes that highlight the importance of resilience and perseverance in the face of adversity. It could inspire readers to keep pushing forward, even when faced with obstacles or setbacks.

4. Finding meaning and fulfillment: "Beyond the Pages" may explore themes related to finding meaning and fulfillment in life. It might provide perspectives on what truly matters, the pursuit of happiness, and living a purposeful life.

5. Appreciating the present moment: Books in this genre often emphasize the significance of being present and mindful in the current moment. They may encourage

readers to appreciate the small joys in life, practice gratitude, and savor each experience.

CHAPTER TWENTY-ONE

Lily Is Back Again..

Once upon a time, in a small town nestled amidst rolling hills, there lived a young woman named Lily. She was a dreamer, always seeking adventure and excitement in the world around her. Lily had always been captivated by the power of stories, but she never quite found the same enchantment in books as others did.

One day, as she wandered through the bustling town square, she stumbled upon a quaint bookstore with a sign that read "Beyond the Pages: Embracing Life's Unwritten Stories" by Adhiraj Narang. Intrigued by the title, Lily stepped inside, her curiosity piqued.

The bookstore was unlike any she had ever seen before. The shelves were filled not only with books but also with colorful journals, blank pages waiting to be filled with untold tales. Lily picked up a copy of "Beyond the Pages" and began to read.

As she turned the pages, she discovered that this book was not like any other she had encountered before. It was not just a collection of stories; it was a guide to embracing the unwritten stories of her own life. Adhiraj Narang's words resonated deeply within her, urging her to step out of her comfort zone and embrace the unknown.

Lily was inspired to embark on a journey of self-discovery and personal growth. She started by writing in one of the blank journals she had found in the store, pouring her thoughts, dreams, and aspirations onto the pages. As she wrote, she realized that her own story was waiting to be written, waiting for her to take the pen and shape it into something extraordinary.

With each passing day, Lily's passion for life grew. She began to explore new hobbies, meet new people, and challenge herself in ways she never thought possible. The book became her constant companion, guiding her through the ups and downs of her journey.

Through "Beyond the Pages," Lily learned the importance of embracing uncertainty and taking risks. She discovered that life's unwritten stories were not to be feared but embraced with open arms. The book taught her that success was not measured by societal standards but by the fulfillment she found in living her own unique story.

As Lily continued to write and live her unwritten story, she realized that reading books, like "Beyond the Pages," had opened up a world of possibilities. It had ignited her imagination, broadened her horizons, and connected her to the hearts and minds of others.

In the end, Lily's story was not just about the book she had read, but about the transformative power of reading itself. It had given her the tools to navigate life's challenges, discover her passions, and embrace the beauty of the unknown.

And so, as Lily closed the final pages of "Beyond the Pages," she knew that her own story would continue to unfold, guided by the wisdom she had gained from the book and the countless stories yet to be discovered.

CHAPTER TWENTY-TWO

Non-Fiction or Fiction Books?

In the vast world of literature, readers are often presented with a choice between non-fiction and fiction books. Both genres offer unique experiences and have their own set of benefits. In this article, we will explore the advantages of reading both non-fiction and fiction books, highlighting why individuals should consider embracing both types of literature.

1. Expanding Knowledge and Understanding:
Non-fiction books are a treasure trove of information, covering a wide range of subjects such as history, science, philosophy, self-help, and more. These books provide readers with valuable knowledge, allowing them to delve into real-world facts and concepts. By reading non-fiction, individuals can expand their understanding of the world, learn new skills, and gain insights from experts in various fields.

2. Gaining New Perspectives:
Fiction books, on the other hand, transport readers to imaginative worlds and offer a unique lens through which

to view society, human nature, and the complexities of life. Through storytelling, fiction allows readers to empathize with diverse characters, experience different cultures, and explore complex emotions. By immersing oneself in fiction, readers can gain fresh perspectives on universal themes, fostering empathy and understanding.

3. Enhancing Creativity and Imagination:
Fiction books stimulate creativity and imagination by presenting readers with vivid descriptions, intricate plots, and engaging narratives. They allow individuals to escape reality temporarily and immerse themselves in imaginative realms where anything is possible. By reading fiction, people can exercise their creative muscles, expand their imagination, and develop their own storytelling abilities.

4. Emotional Connection and Empathy:
Both non-fiction and fiction books have the power to evoke emotions and create a connection between the reader and the subject matter. Non-fiction books can inspire readers through real-life stories of triumph over adversity or offer comfort through shared experiences. Fiction books, meanwhile, enable readers to emotionally invest in characters' lives, fostering empathy and a deeper understanding of human nature.

5. Personal Growth and Self-Reflection:
Both non-fiction and fiction books can contribute to personal growth and self-reflection. Non-fiction books offer guidance, self-help techniques, and insights that can assist individuals in improving themselves and their lives. Fiction books, on the other hand, provide opportunities for introspection and self-discovery by exploring the

complexities of human relationships, personal struggles, and moral dilemmas.

Conclusion:
In conclusion, both non-fiction and fiction books offer unique benefits to readers. Non-fiction expands knowledge, provides insights into real-world subjects, and offers guidance for personal development. Fiction, on the other hand, stimulates creativity, fosters empathy, and provides a platform for self-reflection. Ultimately, the choice between non-fiction and fiction books depends on individual preferences, interests, and the desired reading experience. Embracing both genres can lead to a well-rounded reading journey, broadening one's understanding of the world and enriching personal growth. Thank you Guys and have a great day ahead

CHAPTER TWENTY-THREE

The Power of Writing Books: Why Everyone Should Share Their Stories

As an author, I firmly believe in the transformative power of writing books. While the article may not discuss a specific book titled "Beyond the Pages," it is essential to understand the significance and impact of writing in general. In this piece, we will explore why individuals should embrace the art of writing books and share their stories with the world.

1. Self-Expression and Catharsis:
Writing a book allows individuals to express themselves freely and authentically. It provides an opportunity to delve deep into personal experiences, emotions, and thoughts, offering a cathartic release. By putting our stories on paper, we can gain a better understanding of ourselves, heal emotional wounds, and find closure.

2. Sharing Knowledge and Experiences:
Books are a medium through which we can share our knowledge, expertise, and unique experiences with others. Each person possesses a distinct perspective and life journey that can inspire, educate, or entertain readers. By writing a book, you can contribute to the collective wisdom of humanity, leaving a lasting legacy for future generations.

3. Empowering Others:
Books have the power to influence and empower readers. Your words can touch the lives of individuals who resonate with your story, providing them with solace, motivation, or guidance. By sharing your triumphs, failures, and lessons learned, you can inspire others to overcome their own challenges and reach their full potential.

4. Creating Connection and Understanding:
Books foster empathy and understanding by allowing readers to step into different worlds and perspectives. They bridge gaps between cultures, generations, and social backgrounds, promoting tolerance and compassion. Your book can serve as a catalyst for meaningful conversations, fostering deeper connections among diverse individuals.

5. Personal Growth and Development:
Writing a book is not only about the final product; it is also a transformative journey for the author. The process challenges you intellectually, emotionally, and creatively, fostering personal growth and development. As you research, organize your thoughts, and refine your writing skills, you will evolve as an individual and gain valuable insights along the way.

6. Leaving a Lasting Legacy:
Books have the potential to outlive their authors, creating a lasting impact on future generations. By writing a book, you contribute to the collective human knowledge and leave behind a piece of yourself. Your words can inspire, educate, and entertain for years to come, ensuring that your legacy lives on beyond your lifetime.

Conclusion:
Writing a book is a powerful endeavor that allows individuals to express themselves, share their knowledge, empower others, create connections, and leave a lasting legacy. Regardless of whether the article mentions a specific book or not, the importance of writing and sharing stories cannot be undermined. So, if you have a story within you, I encourage you to embrace the art of writing books and let your voice be heard.

"Beyond the Pages: Challenging the Notion of Reading" is not just a book; it is an invitation to live fully and authentically

As we close the final chapter of this book, let us remember that our stories are not confined to these pages. They are waiting to be written, lived, and shared with the world. So go forth, dear reader, and embrace the unwritten stories that await you.

Conclusion:

In conclusion, "Beyond The Pages: Challenging the Notion of Reading" is a powerful and thought-provoking exploration of the importance of reading in our lives. Adhiraj Narang's book serves as a rallying cry for all those who believe in the transformative power of literature and seek to reignite their love for reading.

Through personal anecdotes, insightful reflections, and practical strategies, Adhiraj inspires readers to break free from the constraints of our fast-paced, technology-driven world and embrace the joy of getting lost in the pages of a well-crafted story. He challenges us to confront the barriers that prevent us from fully engaging with literature and offers guidance on how to overcome them.

"Beyond The Pages" is not just a celebration of reading; it is a call to action. It encourages us to prioritize reading amidst the chaos of our daily lives, to explore different genres, and to engage in meaningful discussions about books. Adhiraj reminds us that reading is not a passive activity but an active process of self-discovery and growth.

By joining Adhiraj on this transformative journey, we can challenge the notion of reading and rediscover the magic that lies within the pages of a book. Together, we can create spaces where reading is celebrated and cherished, and unlock the limitless possibilities that lie beyond the pages.

In a world dominated by technology and instant gratification, "Beyond The Pages" serves as a reminder of the enduring power of literature and the profound impact it can have on our personal growth and understanding of the world. Let us heed its call and embark on a quest to embrace literature, expand our horizons, and reclaim our love for reading.

www.ingramcontent.com/pod-product-compliance
Lightning Source LLC
LaVergne TN
LVHW041122150826
845673LV00007B/2159

* 9 7 9 8 8 9 1 3 3 2 4 6 1 *